What's the Best Little Trivia Book? Volume 2

1,000 Questions About Anything and Everything

David Fickes

Introduction

What you find in most trivia is a lot of erroneous or outdated information or questions that are so simple or esoteric that they aren't interesting. It is difficult to come up with interesting questions that are at the right level of difficulty that a wide variety of people can enjoy them, and they are something that you feel you should know or want to know.

I have tried to ensure that the information is as accurate as possible, and to retain its accuracy, I have also tried to avoid questions whose answers can quickly change with time. Since the simple answer is often not all you want to know, the answers also frequently include additional details to put them in context and provide further information.

There are 1,000 questions about anything and everything. To make it quick and easy to test yourself or others without initially seeing the answers, each page of 25 questions is followed by a page of answers.

If you enjoyed this book and learned a little and would like others to enjoy it also, please put out a review or rating. If you scan the QR code below, it will take you directly to the Amazon review and rating page.

Quiz 1

1) *The Communist Manifesto* was written by what two German philosophers?
2) The process where food browns during cooking is known as what?
3) In what country did Mahatma Gandhi first employ nonviolent civil disobedience to fight for Indian civil rights?
4) How many continents are entirely in the Northern Hemisphere?
5) In terms of mass, what is the most abundant element in the human body?
6) What novel opens with the line "The Mole had been working very hard all the morning, spring-cleaning his little home"?
7) Who was Erich Weiss better known as?
8) What is Europe's longest river?
9) According to USGA rules, how many clubs can a golfer have in their bag?
10) Stonehenge is made of what two main types of rock?
11) What periodic table element has the longest name?
12) What novel has the line "Four legs good, two legs bad"?
13) What book opens with, "Somewhere in la Mancha, in a place whose name I do not care to remember"?
14) In the movie *Life of Pi*, what is the name of the tiger?
15) What is Grandpa Simpson's first name on television's *The Simpsons*?
16) What color are sunsets on Mars?
17) Who first suggested the idea of daylight saving time in an essay he wrote in 1784?
18) What is the only bone in the human body that isn't attached to any other bone?
19) What is the densest planet in our solar system?
20) What is the most common surname in the world?
21) A jellyfish's mouth also serves as what?
22) In Disney's *Snow White and the Seven Dwarfs*, how old is Snow White?
23) What is the second most abundant element in the earth's crust?
24) What is the second-longest river in South America?
25) What is the name for a word with two opposite meanings, such as "clip" that can mean to fasten or detach?

Quiz 1 Answers

1) Karl Marx and Friedrich Engels
2) Maillard reaction
3) South Africa - Gandhi initially fought for the right of the resident Indian community in South Africa. He went to South Africa to work at age 23 and spent 21 years there before returning to India in 1915.
4) Two – Europe and North America
5) Oxygen
6) *The Wind in the Willows* – 1908
7) Harry Houdini
8) Volga – 2,294 miles
9) 14
10) Bluestone and sandstone
11) Rutherfordium
12) *Animal Farm*
13) *Don Quixote*
14) Richard Parker
15) Abraham
16) Blue
17) Benjamin Franklin
18) Hyoid bone – in the throat
19) Earth
20) Chang
21) Anus
22) 14
23) Silicon - 27.7%
24) Parana – 3,032 miles
25) Contronym

Quiz 2

1) What country has the world's highest gambling rate?
2) What was Shakespeare's first play?
3) What was the first sports film to win the Best Picture Oscar?
4) Who is the voice of Marge on television's *The Simpsons*?
5) Where are the Thousand Islands located?
6) What is the capital of the Canadian province of Quebec?
7) Who is the only person to win Olympic gold medals in both indoor and beach volleyball?
8) By area, what is the world's largest gulf?
9) By population, what is the largest city in Australia?
10) What is the highest elevation city to host the Summer Olympics?
11) Based on the number of islands, what is the largest archipelago in the world?
12) Elvis Presley memorized every line from his all-time favorite movie; what was the film?
13) The largest uninhabited island in the world is part of what country?
14) What makes Graca Machel unique among first ladies of the world?
15) What is the most densely populated South American country?
16) What kind of whale is Moby Dick?
17) What mode of transport was invented in 1959 by Armand Bombardier?
18) What is the westernmost U.S. state?
19) The movie *The Magnificent Seven* is based on what 1954 film?
20) What is the division sign (short horizontal line with a dot above and below) in math called?
21) What British prime minister's mother was born in Brooklyn, New York?
22) What is the world's longest mountain range?
23) How many of the 10 most populous countries in the world are in Asia?
24) Who was the first man to set foot on all the continents other than Antarctica?
25) "Bond. James Bond," is first spoken in what film?

Quiz 2 Answers

1) Australia – Over 80% of adults gamble in some form.

2) *Henry VI*

3) *Rocky* – 1976

4) Julie Kavner

5) Saint Lawrence River - They are an archipelago of 1,864 islands between the United States and Canada.

6) Quebec City

7) Karch Kiraly (U.S.) – 1984 and 1988 indoor volleyball gold medals and 1996 beach volleyball gold

8) Gulf of Mexico – 600,000 square miles

9) Sydney

10) Mexico City – 7,350 feet

11) Norwegian Archipelago - at least 240,000 islands, coral reefs, cays, and islets

12) *Patton*

13) Canada - Devon Island in Nunavut Territory is 21,331 square miles at an elevation of 6,300 feet. It is at 75.2 degrees north latitude and is the 27th largest island in the world.

14) First lady of two separate countries – widow of Nelson Mandela (South Africa president) and Samora Machel (Mozambique president)

15) Ecuador

16) Sperm whale

17) Snowmobile

18) Alaska

19) *Seven Samurai*

20) Obelus

21) Winston Churchill

22) Andes – 4,300 miles

23) Seven – China, India, Indonesia, Pakistan, Bangladesh, Russia, Japan

24) Captain James Cook

25) *Dr. No* (1962)– Sean Connery

Quiz 3

1) What is the last event in track and field's decathlon?

2) Hansen's disease is more commonly known as what?

3) What U.S. first lady refused Secret Service coverage and was given her own gun?

4) What was the penalty in ancient Egypt for killing a cat even accidentally?

5) Who was the first man to appear on the cover of *Playboy*?

6) What is the easternmost national capital city in Europe?

7) What movie has disgruntled Korean War veteran Walt Kowalski setting out to reform his neighbor, a Hmong teenager?

8) What are the only two letters that don't appear in any official element names on the periodic table?

9) In what country is the highest point that the equator passes through?

10) What is the largest muscle in the human body?

11) What is Scarlett O'Hara's real first name in *Gone with the Wind*?

12) What is the third-longest river in the United States?

13) Who was the first woman inducted into the Country Music Hall of Fame in 1973?

14) What Central American country extends the furthest north?

15) In 1932, what athlete won the team championship single-handedly at the AAU national track and field meet?

16) What element is named after the creator of dynamite?

17) What was the first U.S. department store?

18) Who had the shortest time in office of any U.S. president who didn't die in office?

19) How many people in modern recorded history have been struck dead by a meteorite?

20) What is the largest species of antelope?

21) What is the only sea without a coastline (no land border)?

22) After calcium, what is the second most abundant mineral in the human body?

23) In Greek mythology, who was the first woman on the earth?

24) *La Giaconda* is better known as what?

25) What didn't President James Buchanan have that every other U.S. president has had?

Quiz 3 Answers

1) 1500 meters
2) Leprosy
3) Eleanor Roosevelt
4) Death
5) Peter Sellers
6) Moscow, Russia - 37.5 degrees east longitude
7) *Gran Torino* - 2008
8) J and Q
9) Ecuador – 15,387 feet
10) Gluteus maximus
11) Katie – Scarlett is her middle name.
12) Yukon River - 1,979 miles starting in British Columbia, Canada, and flowing through Alaska
13) Patsy Cline
14) Belize
15) Mildred "Babe" Didrikson Zaharias - She competed in 8 out of 10 events; she won 5 and tied for first in a sixth event. She won the team championship despite being the only member of her team.
16) Nobelium - named after Alfred Nobel
17) Macy's – 1858
18) Gerald Ford - 895 days
19) One – In 2016 in India, a 40-year-old man was relaxing outside on the grounds of a small engineering college when there was the sound of an explosion; he was found next to a two-foot crater and later succumbed to injuries sustained.
20) Giant eland - They can be almost 6 feet at the shoulder and weigh up to 2,200 pounds.
21) Sargasso Sea – It is in the North Atlantic Ocean off the coast of the United States and is defined by currents.
22) Phosphorus
23) Pandora
24) *Mona Lisa*
25) A wife – He never married, and many historians speculate that he may have been the first gay U.S. president.

Quiz 4

1) What is the coldest national capital city in the world?
2) What is the most populous national capital city in Africa?
3) By area, what is the smallest permanently inhabited U.S. territory?
4) What institution awards the Pulitzer Prizes?
5) Who was the first U.S. citizen to be canonized as a saint?
6) What is the best-selling fiction book of all time?
7) What is painting in watercolor on fresh plaster called?
8) What is the first horror film nominated for the Best Picture Oscar?
9) Other than elephants, what is the heaviest land animal?
10) In what city do the two main tributaries of the Nile River come together?
11) Who has won the most Grammy Awards?
12) What did the Romans call the tenth part of a legion?
13) Who is the writer and director for both *Sleepless in Seattle* and *You've Got Mail*?
14) Who is the only author to publish books in nine of the ten Dewey Decimal categories?
15) What does the human lacrimal gland produce?
16) What country grew the first orange?
17) Who was the first U.S. president to turn 70 while in office?
18) What is the study of plants called?
19) What are the three colors on a roulette wheel?
20) How many witches are in a coven?
21) The land location furthest from any ocean is in what country?
22) What drink did Johann Sebastian Bach enjoy so much that he wrote a cantata for it?
23) What U.S. state has the lowest median age?
24) What is the only U.S. state that borders just one other state?
25) The U.S. Secret Service was created specifically to battle what type of crime?

Quiz 4 Answers

1) Ulaanbaatar, Mongolia – Winter temperatures of minus 40 degrees Fahrenheit are not unusual.
2) Cairo, Egypt
3) American Samoa - 76 square miles
4) Columbia University
5) Mother Frances Xavier Cabrini – 1946
6) *Don Quixote* – estimated 500 million copies
7) Fresco
8) *The Exorcist* – 1973
9) Rhinoceros – up to 8,000 pounds
10) Khartoum, Sudan
11) Beyonce
12) Cohort - 300 to 600 men
13) Nora Ephron
14) Isaac Asimov
15) Tears
16) China
17) Dwight D. Eisenhower - in 1960
18) Botany
19) Black, red, green
20) 13
21) China – 1,645 miles from the ocean near the Kazakhstan border in extreme northwestern China
22) Coffee
23) Utah
24) Maine
25) Counterfeiting - Shortly after the American Civil War, one-third to one-half of all U.S. currency was counterfeit. This was a major threat to the economy, and the Secret Service was founded in 1865 specifically to reduce counterfeiting.

Quiz 5

1) What two mountain ranges did Hannibal and his elephants march through in 218 BC?

2) What is the largest volume lake in Africa?

3) What plant's name comes from the Turkish word for turban?

4) The Pacific Ocean is so large that at some points it is antipodal to itself; what does antipodal mean?

5) What person has the most statues in their honor in the United States?

6) How many eyes do bees have?

7) If you suffer from oniomania, what are you obsessed with?

8) What three sports-related movies have won the Best Picture Oscar?

9) What are the names of Peter Cottontail's sisters in *The Tale of Peter Rabbit*?

10) Who was the first rock star arrested on stage?

11) What standard international unit of power is equal to 1.341 horsepower?

12) What is the only snake that builds a nest?

13) What country consumes the most Coca-Cola per capita?

14) Who appeared in more than 30 Alfred Hitchcock films?

15) Where on the human body are the most sweat glands?

16) Who was the only American in *Monty Python's Flying Circus*?

17) What female alpine skier has the most World Cup downhill season titles?

18) What is the real name of the serial killer known as Son of Sam?

19) After dropping out 34 years earlier, Steven Spielberg got his Bachelor of Arts degree from Cal State Long Beach; what did he submit for credit for his final project in advanced film making?

20) Who is the youngest actor ever nominated for an Oscar?

21) What country has the most United States emigrants?

22) What is the only river that crosses the equator in both a northerly and southerly direction?

23) If you were caught pandiculating, what were you doing?

24) What NHL team set a record for most consecutive playoff appearances with 25 seasons from 1979-2004?

25) What famous actress was one of the inventors of spread spectrum and frequency hopping technology that is the basis for current cellular communications?

Quiz 5 Answers

1) Pyrenees and Alps
2) Lake Tanganyika - Tanzania, DRC, Burundi, and Zambia
3) Tulip
4) Two points are antipodal if they are on diametrically opposite sides of the earth, so at some points in the Pacific Ocean, you could go straight through the center of the earth and come out the other side and still be in the Pacific Ocean.
5) Sacagawea
6) Five
7) Shopping
8) *Rocky*, *Chariots of Fire*, *Million Dollar Baby*
9) Flopsy, Mopsy, Cottontail
10) Jim Morrison - On December 9, 1967, he was arrested as he performed on stage at the New Haven Arena in Connecticut. He was arrested for an incident that took place with a police officer before the show.
11) Kilowatt
12) King cobra – It lays up to 40 eggs at once and builds a nest from vegetation to help keep the eggs safe.
13) Mexico
14) Alfred Hitchcock
15) Bottom of the feet
16) Terry Gilliam
17) Lindsey Vonn – United States
18) David Berkowitz
19) *Schindler's List*
20) Justin Henry – eight years old for *Kramer vs. Kramer*
21) Mexico
22) Congo
23) Stretching and stiffening your trunk and extremities as when fatigued, drowsy, or waking
24) St. Louis Blues
25) Hedy Lamarr - at the beginning of WWII

Quiz 6

1) What was the first car model to sell 20 million units?
2) What is the world's longest freshwater lake?
3) Who was the first American woman to win three gold medals in a single Olympics?
4) What is the only cat species that can't retract its claws?
5) What war did Florence Nightingale tend troops in?
6) How many planets in our solar system have moons?
7) A cat is feline; what kind of animal is leporine?
8) What country contains South America's highest and lowest points?
9) What sports hero wore a cabbage leaf under his cap?
10) Who was the last Major League Baseball player to bat .400?
11) What was the first regularly scheduled broadcast network in the United States?
12) In "The Twelve Days of Christmas," my true love sent to me 10 what?
13) Where did ice hockey originate?
14) After going deaf, what method did Beethoven use to hear almost perfectly?
15) Three U.S. first ladies are tied as the tallest at 5'11"; who are they?
16) In the 19th century, doctors treated hysteria in women by inducing orgasms; what product came out of this?
17) What planet has the strongest winds in our solar system?
18) What is Batman's butler Alfred's last name?
19) When the Persians were at war with the Egyptians, they rounded up and released as many of what animal as they could on the battlefield?
20) What was the family name of the French brothers who were pioneers in hot air ballooning and conducted the first untethered flights?
21) Who is the youngest man to win the Wimbledon tennis singles title?
22) What is the oldest national capital city in Europe?
23) What kind of animal lives in a holt?
24) Easter Island is a territory of what country?
25) What television show has the most Emmy wins for a comedy?

Quiz 6 Answers

1) Volkswagen Beetle
2) Tanganyika – 420 miles in Africa
3) Wilma Rudolph - track and field at the 1960 Rome Olympics
4) Cheetah
5) Crimean
6) Six – Earth, Mars, Jupiter, Saturn, Uranus, Neptune
7) Rabbit
8) Argentina – 22,841 feet above sea level to 344 feet below
9) Babe Ruth – He put chilled cabbage leaves under his cap to keep cool.
10) Ted Williams - 1941
11) NBC – 1945
12) Lords a leaping
13) United Kingdom - There are references to similar games being played on ice in England, Scotland, and Ireland going back 200 years before the first documented game in Canada.
14) Bone conduction - He discovered that if he bit on a metal pole connected to the piano he was playing; he could hear almost perfectly. Vibrations are transferred into our bones, and our ears pick up the signal with no sound distortion, bypassing the eardrums.
15) Melania Trump, Michelle Obama, Eleanor Roosevelt
16) Vibrator
17) Neptune – more than 1,200 mph
18) Pennyworth
19) Cats – Knowing the Egyptians reverence for cats, they knew they would not want to do anything to hurt the cats; the Persians won.
20) Montgolfier
21) Boris Becker – age 17
22) Athens, Greece - founded in about 3000 BC
23) Otter
24) Chile
25) *Frasier* (1993-2004) – 37 wins

Quiz 7

1) Who first wrote about the lost civilization of Atlantis?
2) The rallying cry "Remember the Maine!" came from what war?
3) The word scuba is an acronym for what?
4) What continent has the highest average elevation?
5) How many countries are completely surrounded by one other country?
6) Who was Truman Capote's best friend and next-door neighbor that he first met when he was five years old?
7) What provinces and territories meet at The Four Corners of Canada?
8) What is the most populous island in the world?
9) What ancient measure is the distance from the elbow to the tip of the middle finger?
10) Who wrote the opera *Madam Butterfly*?
11) What famous European writer was captured by Turkish pirates and held as a slave for five years in Algiers?
12) What state was the setting of the Battle of the Little Bighorn?
13) What is the oldest national capital city in South America?
14) Who wrote *Pride and Prejudice*?
15) Gail Borden invented what food item?
16) By area, what is the largest lake in South America?
17) Who was the first U.S. president born in a hospital?
18) A female cat is called a molly; after she has become a mother, what is she called?
19) What U.S. state has the lowest percentage of its area that is water?
20) Who are the only two people to win two Nobel Prizes in two different categories?
21) How many times was Franklin D. Roosevelt elected president?
22) What river flows through Rome?
23) Who was the first American world chess champion?
24) Fort Knox is in what state?
25) What language (not dialect) has the most characters in its alphabet?

Quiz 7 Answers

1) Plato
2) Spanish–American War
3) Self-contained underwater breathing apparatus
4) Antarctica – 8,200 feet average elevation
5) Three – Lesotho (surrounded by South Africa), Vatican City and San Marino (both surrounded by Italy)
6) Harper Lee – author of *To Kill a Mockingbird*
7) Saskatchewan, Manitoba, Northwest Territories, Nunavut
8) Java – Indonesia
9) Cubit
10) Giacomo Puccini
11) Miguel de Cervantes - author of *Don Quixote*
12) Montana
13) Quito, Ecuador - founded in 980 AD
14) Jane Austen
15) Condensed milk
16) Maracaibo – 5,100 square miles
17) Jimmy Carter
18) A queen
19) New Mexico – followed by Arizona and Colorado
20) Marie Curie (1903 Physics and 1911 Chemistry) and Linus Pauling (1954 Chemistry and 1962 Peace)
21) Four - He won the 1932, 1936, 1940, and 1944 elections.
22) Tiber
23) Bobby Fischer
24) Kentucky
25) Cambodian (Khmer) – 74 characters

Quiz 8

1) Macaroni, gentoo, and chinstrap are species of what animal?
2) What is the only U.S. state with a floating post office?
3) What two people appeared separately on the first U.S. postage stamps issued in 1847?
4) In what country did table tennis originate?
5) In what sport are you banned from playing left-handed?
6) Who was on the first postage stamp ever issued in the world?
7) Who are the only two people to win both a Nobel Prize and an Oscar?
8) In what war was "The Charge of the Light Brigade"?
9) Composer Vivaldi had what other profession?
10) Who said, "That which does not kill us makes us stronger"?
11) What is the oldest known name for the island of Great Britain?
12) Who was the first U.S. president to attend Monday night football?
13) Mr. and Mrs. are abbreviations for what?
14) What U.S. television show had the first toilet heard flushing?
15) What color is an aircraft's black box flight recorder?
16) What is the second-longest mountain range in the world?
17) The Statue of Liberty was originally intended for what country?
18) What country has the most volcanoes (active and extinct)?
19) Rats don't sweat; what part of their body do they use to regulate their temperature?
20) *Bambi* was the first Disney film without what?
21) What was the first U.S. television series to feature a final episode where all plot lines were resolved, and all questions were answered?
22) What bathroom staple product was originally called Baby Gays?
23) What country was the first to abolish capital punishment for all crimes?
24) What order of mammals has the most species?
25) What craft requires you to interlace your warp and weft?

Quiz 8 Answers

1) Penguins
2) Michigan – It delivers to ships in Detroit.
3) George Washington and Benjamin Franklin
4) England – late 19th century
5) Polo - If a left-handed and right-handed player went for the ball, they would collide.
6) Queen Victoria - 1840
7) George Bernard Shaw and Bob Dylan
8) Crimean War
9) Priest
10) Friedrich Nietzsche
11) Albion
12) Jimmy Carter
13) Master and mistress
14) *All in the Family* – 1971
15) Orange
16) Rocky Mountains - 3,000 miles through Canada and United States
17) Egypt – They rejected it.
18) United States – 173
19) Tail - They constrict or expand blood vessels in their tails.
20) Human characters
21) *The Fugitive* - 1967
22) Q-tips
23) Venezuela - by constitution in 1863
24) Rodents
25) Weaving

Quiz 9

1) What country has the southernmost university in the world?
2) Written out in English, what is the first number that contains the letter a?
3) By mass, what is the smallest known mammal?
4) What is the heaviest North American flying bird?
5) "Fidelity, Bravery, and Integrity" is what U.S. organization's motto?
6) The United States has the most Nobel Prize winners in history; what country is second?
7) Who is the arch-enemy of Austin Powers?
8) What bird can only eat when its head is upside down?
9) What is the name for a group of giraffes?
10) Based on the number of members, what country has the largest legislature in the world?
11) What is the world's busiest airport based on passenger traffic?
12) What is the largest desert in the world?
13) What African country was divided in two in 2011?
14) What pandemic beginning in 541 AD is believed to be the first significant occurrence of the bubonic plague?
15) What country's only land border is with Germany?
16) What is the name for the part of the human ear that receives sound vibrations and converts them into nerve impulses?
17) What country was Mother Teresa born in?
18) What is the standard international unit of force?
19) What film has the insult "Your mother was a hamster, and your father smelt of elderberries"?
20) What is the name for a group of hummingbirds?
21) What Spanish soldier of fortune led the expedition that discovered the Pacific Ocean?
22) In which Winter Olympics team sport is pebbling part of the preparation?
23) What were the surnames of Bonnie and Clyde?
24) What film character said, "I just put one foot in front of the other. When I get tired, I sleep. When I get hungry, I eat. When I have to go to the bathroom, I go"?
25) What is the singular of graffiti?

Quiz 9 Answers

1) Argentina - National University of Tierra del Fuego in Ushuaia, Argentina, at 54.8 degrees south latitude

2) One thousand

3) Etruscan shrew - On average, they weigh about 0.06 ounces. It also has the fastest heartbeat of any mammal at 1,500 beats per minute.

4) Trumpeter swan - up to 38 pounds

5) FBI

6) United Kingdom

7) Dr. Evil

8) Flamingo

9) Tower

10) China - The National People's Congress is a single house made up of 2,980 members.

11) Atlanta, Georgia

12) Antarctic Polar Desert – 5.5 million square miles

13) Sudan – now Sudan and South Sudan

14) Justinian Plague - It is estimated to have killed 25-50 million people over the following two centuries of recurrence.

15) Denmark

16) Cochlea

17) Macedonia

18) Newton – One newton equals the force needed to accelerate one kilogram of mass at the rate of one meter per second squared.

19) *Monty Python and the Holy Grail*

20) Charm

21) Vasco Balboa

22) Curling - Pebbling the ice is done to create friction for the stone to curl; they sprinkle the ice with tiny water droplets that freeze on the surface to create a pebbled texture.

23) Clyde Barrow and Bonnie Parker

24) Forrest Gump

25) Graffito

Quiz 10

1) What was Stephen King's first published novel?
2) What was the original name for the island where the Statue of Liberty stands?
3) What was the first U.S. consumer product sold in the former Soviet Union?
4) In the movie *The Day the Earth Stood Still*, what is the name of the alien?
5) What is the name for the dark gray color the eyes see in perfect darkness because of optic nerve signals?
6) What is Barbie the doll's full name?
7) Who was the shortest U.S. president?
8) The fennec is the smallest species of what animal?
9) Who is the Bluetooth wireless technology named after?
10) Who was the first celebrity to make a guest appearance on television's *Sesame Street*?
11) Where did two jumbo jets collide in 1977, killing 579?
12) Who is the oldest person to host television's *Saturday Night Live*?
13) What is the highest level of sociality called where animals like ants have a single female or caste that produces the offspring, and nonreproductive individuals cooperate in caring for the young?
14) What singles figure skater has won the most U.S. Championships?
15) William Moulton Marston created the *Wonder Woman* character and was also a psychologist and inventor of what well-known device?
16) Sideburns are named after what American Civil War general?
17) What did Robert Heft design in 1958 as a part of a high school history class project?
18) What country has on average the tallest people?
19) What was the first U.S. state?
20) Camels don't store water in their humps; where do they store it?
21) Based on oxygen usage, what animal is the most efficient swimmer?
22) Who was the target of the first known attempted assassination of a U.S. president?
23) On a QWERTY keyboard, what two letters have raised marks to assist with touch typing?
24) Who was the first U.S. president born outside the original 13 states?
25) Who invented the exploding shell?

Quiz 10 Answers

1) *Carrie*
2) Bedloe's Island
3) Pepsi
4) Klaatu
5) Eigengrau
6) Barbara Millicent Roberts
7) James Madison – 5'4"
8) Fox - They are found mainly in the Sahara and elsewhere in North Africa; they only weigh two to three pounds but have six-inch ears.
9) King Harald "Bluetooth" Gormsson – He ruled Denmark in the 10th century.
10) James Earl Jones – He appeared on the show's second episode.
11) Tenerife, Canary Islands
12) Betty White – 88
13) Eusocial
14) Dick Button - seven consecutive from 1946-1952
15) Lie detector – consequently, Wonder Woman's Lasso of Truth
16) Ambrose Burnside - He was known for having an unusual facial hairstyle with a mustache connected to thick sideburns with a clean-shaven chin.
17) Current 50-star U.S. flag
18) Netherlands – an average of 6'½" for men and 5'7" for women
19) Delaware – December 7, 1787
20) Bloodstream - They can drink up to 20 gallons at a time; the hump is almost all fat and serves as an alternative energy source and helps regulate body temperature. By concentrating fat in the hump as opposed to being spread over their body, they are better able to handle hot climates.
21) Jellyfish – It uses 48% less oxygen than any other known animal; they never stop moving.
22) Andrew Jackson - In 1835, he was attending the funeral of South Carolina congressman Warren R. Davis when Richard Lawrence fired two pistols at point-blank range; both misfired.
23) F and J
24) Abraham Lincoln
25) Henry Shrapnel

Quiz 11

1) By area, what is the fourth largest continent?
2) What famous philosopher was a two-time winner at the ancient Olympics?
3) What are the three main parts of an insect's body?
4) What year were the first modern Olympics held?
5) What movie sold the most tickets of all time in the United States?
6) What is the ancient practice of trying to protect yourself against poisoning by taking non-lethal doses of poison to build immunity called?
7) What is the oldest hamburger restaurant chain in the United States?
8) What country's only land border is with Saudi Arabia?
9) Why do pen caps have a hole in them?
10) What was the third country to develop an atomic bomb?
11) In the novel *Little Women*, what is the surname of the sisters?
12) What was the first U.S. state to legalize same-sex marriage?
13) What country won the first men's soccer World Cup?
14) Which U.S. first lady was the first to earn a postgraduate degree?
15) What is the only country in the world without an official capital?
16) What is the only animal that naturally has an odd number of whiskers?
17) Who was the first American to win the Tour de France bicycle race?
18) What male athlete has the most career Winter Olympic medals?
19) What national capital city has views of the volcano Snaefellsjokull?
20) What is it called when you mishear or misinterpret a phrase in a way that gives it a new meaning, such as when you mishear the lyrics of a song and insert words that sound similar and make sense?
21) What is the only U.S. state name that can be typed on one row of a standard keyboard?
22) Who duplicated Jesse Owens' feat by winning four track and field Olympic gold medals in 1984?
23) By area, what is the largest country with Spanish as an official language?
24) Who was the first MLB player to hit 400 home runs and steal 400 bases?
25) What was the occupation of the first person to propose the big bang origin of the universe?

Quiz 11 Answers

1) South America

2) Plato - He won in pankration, which was a submission sport combining elements of wrestling and boxing but with very few rules; only eye-gouging and biting were banned.

3) Head, thorax, and abdomen

4) 1896 – Athens

5) *Gone with the Wind* – About 208 million tickets have been sold; the U.S. population in 1939 when it was released was 131 million.

6) Mithridatism - From the end of the 1st century AD, Roman emperors adopted the daily habit of taking a small amount of every known poison to gain immunity. It can be effective against some types of poisons, but depending on the poison, it can lead to a lethal accumulation in the body over time.

7) White Castle – It was founded in 1921 in Wichita, Kansas; the original hamburger slider was 5 cents.

8) Qatar

9) Prevent suffocation in case they are swallowed

10) Great Britain

11) March

12) Massachusetts - 2004

13) Uruguay – 1930

14) Hillary Clinton

15) Nauru – It is the third-smallest country in the world in the Central Pacific Ocean.

16) Catfish

17) Greg Lemond – 1986

18) Ole Einar Bjorndalen (Norway) - 13 biathlon medals from 1998-2014

19) Reykjavik, Iceland

20) Mondegreen

21) Alaska

22) Carl Lewis – He won the 100, 200, 4 x 100, and long jump

23) Argentina

24) Barry Bonds - 1998

25) Priest – Georges Lemaitre

Quiz 12

1) Who first wrote, "Do not count your chickens before they are hatched"?
2) What country gained its independence from Denmark in 1944?
3) In *Willy Wonka and the Chocolate Factory*, what is the last name of the protagonist Charlie?
4) What is Europe's second-longest river?
5) What is the longest river in the world that flows entirely within one country?
6) What is the second-largest island in Europe?
7) What is the only U.S. state with a one-syllable name?
8) Tenochtitlan was the capital of what empire?
9) If you exclude Vatican City as a national capital, what pair of national capital cities are closest together?
10) What tiny vessel connects an artery with a vein?
11) Ageusia is the loss of what sense?
12) What international best-selling author also wrote under the name Mary Westmacott?
13) What is Lake Kinneret known as in the Bible?
14) What is the longest tributary river in the world?
15) What sport features the fastest moving ball?
16) What U.S. president died at the youngest age?
17) Who was the first woman to win a Nobel Prize?
18) Who was the first American woman to win the Olympic women's gymnastics all-around gold medal?
19) What national capital rises where the Blue Nile and White Nile converge?
20) What did English Queen Mary II die of at age 32?
21) What animal has the longest tongue?
22) What South American country has Pacific and Atlantic coastlines?
23) What is the only Southeast Asian country never colonized by Europeans?
24) What single sporting event has the most in-person spectators in the world?
25) In math, what does a "lemniscate" shape mean?

Quiz 12 Answers

1) Aesop – *The Milkmaid and Her Pail*
2) Iceland
3) Bucket
4) Danube – 1,777 miles
5) Yangtze - 3,964 miles entirely in China
6) Iceland – 39,702 square miles
7) Maine
8) Aztec
9) Brazzaville, Republic of the Congo, and Kinshasa, Democratic Republic of the Congo - two miles apart
10) Capillary
11) Taste
12) Agatha Christie
13) Sea of Galilee
14) Irtysh River - 2,640 miles in Russia, China, and Kazakhstan. It is the chief tributary of the Ob River.
15) Jai-alai – up to 188 mph
16) John F. Kennedy – 46
17) Marie Curie
18) Mary Lou Retton - 1984 Los Angeles
19) Khartoum, Sudan
20) Smallpox
21) Blue whale - about 18 feet long
22) Colombia
23) Thailand
24) Tour de France bicycle race - 12 to 15 million
25) Infinity - Lemniscate is a shape with two loops meeting at a central point.

Quiz 13

1) At the start of the 20th century, how many U.S. states were there?
2) On television's *Seinfeld*, what is Kramer's first name?
3) What fish's skin was once used commercially as sandpaper?
4) Who plays the character whose dismembered body is fed into the wood chipper in the movie *Fargo*?
5) What state's highest point is Mount Rainier?
6) What U.S. state has the highest percentage of its area that is water?
7) What is the highest mountain in Europe?
8) Who was the first African American U.S. Supreme Court justice?
9) What is the highest male singing voice called?
10) How many prime numbers are there that are less than 20?
11) After his defeat at Waterloo, Napoleon spent the last six years of his life under British supervision on what island?
12) What was the profession of serial killer Ted Bundy?
13) What is the only movie Alfred Hitchcock made twice?
14) What is the name for a castrated rooster?
15) What is Tarzan's real identity?
16) Who was the first English monarch to live in Buckingham Palace?
17) What empire lasted from 1324 to 1922?
18) In what country was Nutella invented?
19) What unit of measure is equal to about 3.26 light-years?
20) What species is the oldest living individual tree?
21) What did the acronym ESPN (television network) originally stand for?
22) What element has the symbol Pb?
23) What country has the highest per capita electricity consumption?
24) If an animal is edentulous, what is it lacking?
25) What is the most populous city south of the equator?

Quiz 13 Answers

1) 45 – Oklahoma, New Mexico, Arizona, Alaska, and Hawaii weren't states yet.
2) Cosmo
3) Shark
4) Steve Buscemi
5) Washington - 14,417 feet
6) Michigan – followed by Hawaii and Rhode Island
7) Mount Elbrus - 18,510 feet in Russia
8) Thurgood Marshall - 1967
9) Countertenor
10) Eight numbers - 2, 3, 5, 7, 11, 13, 17, 19
11) St. Helena - It is 1,162 miles off the west coast of Africa in the South Atlantic.
12) Attorney
13) *The Man Who Knew Too Much* – 1934 and 1956
14) Capon
15) Lord Greystoke
16) Queen Victoria - 1837
17) Ottoman or Turkish Empire
18) Italy – In 1946, an Italian pastry maker was looking for a cheaper alternative to chocolate that was in short supply due to WWII, so he mixed hazelnuts with some cocoa.
19) Parsec
20) Bristlecone pine - 5,000 years
21) Entertainment and Sports Programming Network
22) Lead - Pb comes from the Latin word "plumbum," meaning waterworks; in ancient times, lead was widely used in the construction of water pipes.
23) Iceland – more than four times higher than the United States
24) Teeth
25) Sao Paulo, Brazil

Quiz 14

1) In the book of Genesis in the Bible, what did God create on the fourth day?
2) Who wrote *The Man in the Iron Mask*?
3) What national capital city is closest to the equator?
4) What American statesman wrote the collection of essays *Fart Proudly*?
5) What country has the oldest parliament in the world?
6) What Ridley Scott film about two female best friends is one of the very few films ever to produce two Best Actress Oscar nominations?
7) By area, what is the smallest continent?
8) Who wrote *The Call of the Wild*?
9) What is the second-longest river in Asia?
10) What is the name of the mascot depicted as a portly older man with a mustache, suit, bowtie, and top hat in the game Monopoly?
11) What is the most common symbol on flags of the world?
12) What was the first movie to make $100 million at the box office?
13) Who wrote, "How do I love thee? Let me count the ways"?
14) What is the name for a group of porcupines?
15) What show had the first interracial couple on regular primetime U.S. television?
16) What is the only African country that borders the Mediterranean Sea and the Atlantic Ocean?
17) What war caused the most American deaths?
18) The term caprine relates to what kind of animals?
19) What is the only king in a standard card deck of cards that doesn't have a mustache?
20) What is the longest river in North America?
21) What ship collided with the Swedish liner *Stockholm* on July 26, 1956?
22) Alexander the Great was king of what country?
23) What is the most abundant element in the earth's crust?
24) In 1917, Germany invited what country to join WWI by attacking the United States to recover lost territories?
25) By area, what is the third-largest U.S. state?

Quiz 14 Answers

1) Sun, moon, and stars
2) Alexandre Dumas
3) Quito, Ecuador - 15.9 miles south of the equator
4) Benjamin Franklin
5) Iceland - 930
6) *Thelma & Louise* - 1991
7) Australia
8) Jack London
9) Yellow – 3,395 miles
10) Rich Uncle Pennybags - He was inspired by tycoon J.P. Morgan.
11) Star
12) *Jaws*
13) Elizabeth Barrett Browning
14) Prickle
15) *The Jeffersons* - neighbors Tom and Helen Willis in 1975
16) Morocco
17) American Civil War
18) Goats
19) King of hearts
20) Missouri – 2,341 miles
21) *Andrea Doria*
22) Macedonia
23) Oxygen - 46.6%
24) Mexico
25) California

Quiz 15

1) What did Starbucks only sell when it started?
2) What game has the most books written about it?
3) What is the second deepest lake in the world?
4) In movies, what is Dirty Harry's last name?
5) Who has been on the cover of *Time* magazine more times than any other person?
6) By discharge volume, what is the largest river in the world?
7) What continent stretches from the equator to the Arctic Circle?
8) Who was the only U.S. president who was a licensed bartender?
9) What mountain range is Mount Kilimanjaro part of?
10) What was the first sport to be filmed?
11) What did Russian Valentina Tereshkova become the first woman to do in 1963?
12) Who was the first African American to win the Wimbledon men's singles tennis title?
13) Who was the first NHL player to score 100 points in six consecutive seasons?
14) What is the northernmost national capital city in Africa?
15) By area, what is the largest lake in Europe?
16) By area, what is the fourth-largest U.S. state?
17) What country eats the most chocolate per capita?
18) Wisconsin isn't known as the Badger State because of the animal. Miners in the 1830s lived in temporary caves cut into the hillsides that became known as badger dens, and the miners who lived in them were known as badgers; what were they mining?
19) Even though it makes up about 2.4% of the earth's crust, what element is never found in its pure form in nature?
20) Who is the only U.S. president who did not represent a political party when he was elected?
21) Who is the only person to win an Olympic gold medal and an Oscar?
22) What date was the Declaration of Independence signed?
23) Who played Rooster Cogburn in the 2010 *True Grit* movie remake?
24) Who is the only NBA player to win MVP, defensive player of the year, and Finals MVP in the same year?
25) Of all the players in North American men's professional sports, who has won the most MVP awards?

Quiz 15 Answers

1) Whole roasted coffee beans
2) Chess
3) Lake Tanganyika - 4,820 feet deep in southeastern Africa
4) Callahan
5) Richard Nixon - 55 appearances
6) Amazon
7) Asia
8) Abraham Lincoln
9) None – At 19,340 feet, it is the highest mountain in the world that isn't part of a range.
10) Boxing - 1894
11) Travel in space
12) Arthur Ashe
13) Bobby Orr - 1969 to 1975
14) Tunis, Tunisia - 36.8 degrees north latitude
15) Ladoga – 6,834 square miles in Russia
16) Montana - 147,040 square miles
17) Switzerland
18) Lead
19) Potassium – It is so reactive that it is never found in its pure form in nature; it must be isolated artificially by separating it from its compounds.
20) George Washington
21) Kobe Bryant – Olympic basketball gold medals in 2008 and 2012 and Best Animated Short Film for *Dear Basketball* in 2018
22) August 2, 1776 - It was adopted on July 4, 1776, but wasn't signed until August.
23) Jeff Bridges
24) Hakeem Olajuwon
25) Wayne Gretzky – nine

Quiz 16

1) Who wrote *Crime and Punishment*?

2) A positive number that equals the sum of its divisors excluding itself is called what?

3) Who wrote the Father Brown crime stories?

4) What is the only crime defined in the U.S. Constitution?

5) What U.S. state has the smallest population?

6) Who was the only Eagle Scout U.S. president?

7) What recurring character on television's *The Simpsons* is voiced by Kelsey Grammer?

8) What science fiction movie was originally made in 1956 and remade in 1978 and 1993?

9) What is the only animal with four forward-facing knees?

10) What drug was introduced by Bayer in 1898 and marketed as a non-addicting alternative to morphine and a treatment for cough inducing illnesses like bronchitis?

11) A male horse and a female donkey produce what offspring?

12) Who was the editor of the magazine *Babies Just Babies* when her husband was elected U.S. president?

13) What U.S. state capital has the largest population?

14) Who holds the NBA record for most career free throws made?

15) "Pay no attention to that man behind the curtain," is from what classic movie?

16) What was the first European country to create national parks?

17) The physiological sense called equilibrioception is known by what more common term?

18) What is the capital of Mongolia?

19) What are the names of the two rival department stores in the movie *Miracle on 34th Street*?

20) What country is the fourth largest in the Americas (North and South America)?

21) Who wrote *The Wonderful Wizard of Oz*?

22) What is the only planet in our solar system less dense than water?

23) What non-landlocked country has the shortest coastline?

24) What is the deepest river in Asia?

25) On the periodic table, what is the first element alphabetically?

Quiz 16 Answers

1) Fyodor Dostoevsky
2) Perfect number
3) G.K. Chesterton
4) Treason - Article III, Section 3
5) Wyoming
6) Gerald Ford
7) Sideshow Bob
8) *Invasion of the Body Snatchers*
9) Elephant - All other four-legged animals have at least one pair of legs with knees that face backward.
10) Heroin - The AMA approved it for general use in 1906 and recommended it as a morphine replacement; soon, there were 200,000 heroin addicts in New York City alone.
11) Hinny
12) Eleanor Roosevelt
13) Phoenix, Arizona
14) Karl Malone - 9,787
15) *The Wizard of Oz* – 1939
16) Sweden - 1909
17) Sense of balance
18) Ulaanbaatar
19) Macy's and Gimbels
20) Argentina
21) L. Frank Baum
22) Saturn
23) Monaco – 2.4 miles
24) Yangtze - 656 feet maximum depth, 2nd deepest in the world
25) Actinium

Quiz 17

1) What U.S. state has the fewest counties?
2) What is the largest island in the Pacific Ocean?
3) Where did curling originate?
4) What is the smallest organ in the human body?
5) What is the fleshy protuberance above a turkey's bill called?
6) What three states share Yellowstone National Park?
7) What mythic character rode horses called Llamrei and Hengroen?
8) What letter begins the fewest words in the English language?
9) The heat of chili peppers is measured in what?
10) What two countries share Victoria Falls in Africa?
11) Tempera paint's primary ingredients are water and what?
12) What country has the largest Spanish-speaking population?
13) What was the first instant coffee?
14) What name is given to a female mouse?
15) Of all the countries that celebrate an independence day, the largest number gained independence from what country?
16) In the human body, what is produced by the parotid glands?
17) What do polled cattle not have?
18) What country is bordered by Belgium, France, and Germany?
19) What is the deepest gorge in the United States?
20) What is the only land mammal native to New Zealand?
21) On average, what is the coldest planet in our solar system?
22) How many fillies have won the Kentucky Derby?
23) What state had the first commercial oil well in the United States?
24) What is the male part of a flower called?
25) What U.S. state has the most counties?

Quiz 17 Answers

1) Delaware – three
2) New Guinea - 303,476 square miles
3) Scotland
4) Pineal gland – in the center of the brain
5) Snood
6) Wyoming (96%), Montana (3%), Idaho (1%)
7) King Arthur
8) X
9) Scoville Heat Units
10) Zambia and Zimbabwe
11) Egg yolk
12) Mexico
13) Nescafe
14) Doe
15) Great Britain (58) - followed by France (26), Russia (21), Spain (21)
16) Saliva
17) Horns
18) Luxembourg
19) Hells Canyon – 7,993 feet deep on the Snake River on the Oregon and Idaho border
20) Bat
21) Neptune – minus 353 degrees Fahrenheit
22) Three - 1915, 1980, 1988
23) Pennsylvania
24) Stamen
25) Texas – 254

Quiz 18

1) What animal has the most taste buds?
2) Anthony Daniels played what character in a series of films?
3) What modern word comes from a knight who was free for hire?
4) In what Shakespeare play does the character Caliban appear?
5) Who was the only U.S. president who had been a union leader?
6) Who was America's first public enemy number one?
7) Who was the first American to win the Olympic marathon gold medal?
8) What was bubble wrap originally intended to be used for?
9) While there are more than 60 species of eagles worldwide, how many species live in North America?
10) What species of animal (not microscopic) has the largest size difference between males and females?
11) Who is the only NBA player with 40 points and 40 rebounds in a game?
12) Who was the first actor or actress to reject their Oscar win?
13) Who are the only two actresses who have won consecutive Best Actress Oscars?
14) Who was vice president when Abraham Lincoln was assassinated?
15) Who was offered the presidency of Israel in 1952 and turned it down?
16) What is the largest peninsula in the world?
17) In the movie *Close Encounters of the Third Kind*, what is the real location that Richard Dreyfuss' character builds in mashed potatoes and is drawn to?
18) Who wrote a series of novels about CIA analyst Jack Ryan?
19) *The Imitation Game* is set during WWII and stars Benedict Cumberbatch as what real-life mathematical genius?
20) What was the name of the royal house that ruled Russia from 1613 to 1917?
21) What is the southernmost urban area in the world with a population of over 20 million?
22) In the 48 contiguous U.S. states, what is the most western state capital?
23) What is a digamy?
24) How many states border the Great Lakes?
25) Who wrote, "A thing of beauty is a joy for ever"?

Quiz 18 Answers

1) Catfish – It has over 100,000 taste buds both in its mouth and all over its body, about 10 times more than humans.

2) C–3PO – *Star Wars*

3) Freelance

4) *The Tempest*

5) Ronald Reagan – president of the Screen Actors Guild

6) John Dillinger

7) Frank Shorter – 1972

8) Wallpaper

9) Two - bald eagle and golden eagle

10) Blanket octopus – Females are 10,000 to 40,000 times larger than males; females can be 6.5 feet in length; males are 1 inch.

11) Wilt Chamberlain - 1968

12) George C. Scott – 1971 for *Patton*

13) Luise Rainer – *The Great Ziegfeld* (1936) and *The Good Earth* (1937) and Katharine Hepburn – *Guess Who's Coming to Dinner* (1967) and *The Lion in Winter* (1968)

14) Andrew Johnson

15) Albert Einstein

16) Arabian Peninsula - 1,250,006 square miles

17) Devils Tower National Monument in Wyoming

18) Tom Clancy

19) Alan Turing

20) Romanov

21) Sao Paulo, Brazil - 23.9 degrees south latitude

22) Olympia, Washington

23) A second legal marriage after death or divorce

24) Eight - Illinois, Indiana, Michigan, Minnesota, New York, Ohio, Pennsylvania, Wisconsin

25) John Keats

Quiz 19

1) What country makes the most films per year?
2) What country eats the most macaroni and cheese per capita?
3) What country has the most active volcanoes?
4) What country has the largest area of inland waters?
5) What is the most populous national capital city in Europe?
6) What musical term means to play a piece of music lively and fast?
7) Who wrote *The Chronicles of Narnia*?
8) What international movie star was born in a bombed-out French village during WWI?
9) What is the first prime number after 1,000,000?
10) Which of the seven dwarfs comes first alphabetically?
11) What country has the northernmost university in the world?
12) What was the first product to have a barcode?
13) In *Star Trek*, what is the name of Spock's father?
14) What is the second-largest rodent in the world?
15) Who wrote *Robinson Crusoe*?
16) By area, what is the largest of the Canadian provinces and territories?
17) What animal lives in a drey?
18) Including hunting dives, what is the fastest bird in the world?
19) Who wrote *The Wind in the Willows*?
20) What is the longest U.S. state from north to south?
21) What is the name of the island between the two waterfalls at Niagara Falls?
22) What future U.S. president delivered an 84-minute campaign speech after being shot just before the event?
23) What country has the most countries or territories bordering it?
24) What is the national animal of the United States?
25) Based on the number of weeks at number one on Billboard's Hot 100, who was the top artist of the 2000s?

Quiz 19 Answers

1) India
2) Canada
3) Indonesia – 76 active volcanoes
4) Canada
5) Moscow, Russia
6) Allegro
7) C.S. Lewis
8) Rin Tin Tin
9) 1,000,003
10) Bashful
11) Norway - University of Tromsø in Tromsø, Norway, at 69.7 degrees north latitude
12) Wrigley's gum
13) Sarek
14) North American beaver - up to 110 pounds
15) Daniel Defoe
16) Nunavut – 808,200 square miles
17) Squirrel
18) Peregrine falcon – 242 mph
19) Kenneth Grahame
20) Alaska – 1,479 miles
21) Goat Island
22) Theodore Roosevelt - He was shot as he stood up in an open-air automobile and waved his hat to the crowd. X-rays taken after the speech showed the bullet lodged against Roosevelt's fourth right rib on an upward path toward his heart.
23) China – 14 countries and 2 territories
24) Bison
25) Usher

Quiz 20

1) Who was the first U.S. president who was a lawyer?

2) What country has the highest minimum elevation?

3) Who is generally credited with inventing the television as we know it and giving the world's first public demonstration of a true television set?

4) What is a baby owl called?

5) In what country or territory is the northernmost point of land in the world?

6) What name is mentioned most in the Bible?

7) What is the only Asian country the equator passes through?

8) Who was the first player in MLB history to steal 100 bases in a season?

9) Who is the youngest solo artist to have a number-one hit on Billboard's Hot 100?

10) After *Sleeping Beauty* in 1959, what was the next fairy tale produced by Disney?

11) What was the first U.S. men's professional sport to have female referees for regular season play?

12) What two planets in our solar system rotate clockwise?

13) What is the first film by a black director to win the Best Picture Oscar?

14) The word goodbye is a contraction of what phrase?

15) What country has the longest national anthem?

16) What is the smallest animal that represents a year in the Chinese zodiac?

17) Lexico was the original name for what popular board game?

18) Who was the first U.S. president to receive the Purple Heart?

19) Who is the only golfer to complete a calendar-year Grand Slam?

20) What is the second hardest gem after diamond?

21) In horse racing, which of the Triple Crown races is the shortest?

22) What country has the longest coastline in Asia?

23) What is the longest U.S. interstate highway?

24) How many of the Beatles could read or write music?

25) What is the least densely populated North American country?

Quiz 20 Answers

1) John Adams
2) Lesotho - 4,593 feet minimum elevation
3) John Logie Baird - He demonstrated a television set in 1926.
4) Owlet
5) Greenland - Kaffeklubben Island (Coffee Club Island) is a small island off the northern tip of Greenland at 83.7 degrees north latitude.
6) David – followed by Jesus
7) Indonesia
8) Maury Wills – 104 steals in 1962
9) Stevie Wonder – age 13 with "Fingertips Part 2" in 1963
10) *The Little Mermaid* – 1989
11) NBA - 1997
12) Venus and Uranus
13) *12 Years a Slave* - 2013
14) God be with ye.
15) Greece - Its national anthem, "Hymn to Liberty," has 158 verses. The anthem is a poem written in 1823 by Dionysios Solomos and set to music by Nikolaos Mantzaros.
16) Rat
17) Scrabble
18) John F. Kennedy
19) Bobby Jones – 1930
20) Sapphire
21) Preakness – 1 3/16 miles
22) Indonesia - 33,939 miles
23) I-90 from Boston to Seattle – 3,111 miles
24) None - When they needed to write music for others to play, arrangers at sheet music publishing companies would do it.
25) Canada

Quiz 21

1) What country has the world's tallest vertical cliff?
2) What is Dorothy's last name in *The Wizard of Oz*?
3) The Fields Medal is awarded for achievement in what field?
4) In the movie, what book does Forrest Gump keep in his suitcase?
5) Who is the Danish explorer who gave his name to a strait, sea, island, glacier, and land bridge?
6) Edmond Dantes is better known as what literary hero?
7) In what city did Rosa Parks refuse to give up her seat?
8) What piece of sporting equipment has a maximum length of 42 inches and a maximum diameter of 2.61 inches?
9) What U.S. Constitutional amendment granted women the right to vote?
10) In Disney's *Snow White and the Seven Dwarfs*, what do the dwarfs mine?
11) Who is the first character to speak in the movie *Star Wars*?
12) Up until 1954, what color were U.S. traffic stop signs?
13) What U.S. president married his teacher?
14) Who wrote *The Glass Menagerie*?
15) Lettuce is a member of what plant family?
16) What U.S. state has the most colleges?
17) Who was the first U.S. president to govern over all 50 states?
18) What author created more than 1,700 of our common English words, more than any other person?
19) What country issued the first Christmas stamp in 1898?
20) What title has been won by the rider who wears the polka dot jersey in the Tour de France?
21) What Dr. Seuss tale is set "on the 15th of May, in the jungle of Nool, in the heat of the day, in the cool of the pool"?
22) What is the fastest swimming fish?
23) What is the largest species of monkey?
24) After the sun, what is the closest star to the earth?
25) Which of the 48 contiguous U.S. states extends farthest north?

Quiz 21 Answers

1) Canada – Mount Thor on Baffin Island with a 4,101 feet vertical drop
2) Gale
3) Mathematics
4) *Curious George*
5) Vitus Bering
6) Count of Monte Cristo
7) Montgomery, Alabama
8) Baseball bat
9) 19th
10) Diamonds
11) C-3PO
12) Yellow
13) Millard Fillmore - Fillmore's first wife, Abigail Powers, was his teacher when he was 19 years old.
14) Tennessee Williams
15) Sunflower
16) Texas
17) Dwight D. Eisenhower
18) William Shakespeare - He did it by changing nouns into verbs, changing verbs into adjectives, connecting words never used together, adding prefixes and suffixes, and creating original words; he also created many common phrases. Some examples of his creations include fancy-free, lie low, foregone conclusion, a sorry sight, for goodness sake, good riddance, dishearten, eventful, new-fangled, hot-blooded, rant, laughable, a wild goose chase.
19) Canada
20) King of the Mountains
21) *Horton Hears a Who!*
22) Sailfish – 68 mph
23) Mandrill - They are found mostly in tropical rainforests in southern Cameroon, Gabon, Equatorial Guinea, and the Congo and can be up to 120 pounds.
24) Proxima Centauri - 4.22 light-years away
25) Minnesota

Quiz 22

1) What is the largest island in the Atlantic Ocean?
2) What war did Joan of Arc's inspirational leadership help end?
3) What is the U.S. national tree?
4) What U.S. state has the most miles of rivers?
5) Who established the science of genetics in 1866?
6) What romantic comedy has the line "I'll have what she's having"?
7) In the movie *Slumdog Millionaire*, what is the final answer Jamal gives to win the grand prize?
8) What movie has the line "You're gonna need a bigger boat"?
9) What is the most used letter in the English alphabet?
10) Orienteering began in what country?
11) Whose autobiography was *The Long Walk to Freedom*?
12) What country is bordered by France, Italy, Austria, and Germany?
13) What is the best-selling science fiction book of all time?
14) Adjusted for inflation, what is the only horror film to gross $1 billion in the United States?
15) What is the capital of the Canadian province of British Columbia?
16) What two U.S. state capitals include the name of the state?
17) Who made the first solo round the world flight?
18) What is the only human internal organ that can regenerate itself?
19) By area, what is the largest Scandinavian country?
20) Practiced between the 5th and 16th centuries, what was a poetic exchange of insults called?
21) By population, what is the largest city at least partly in Europe?
22) Joel and Ethan Coen's movie *O Brother, Where Art Thou?* is loosely based on what ancient epic poem?
23) Who organized the Boston Tea Party?
24) Not including insects and crustaceans, what are the only two animals that can see completely behind themselves without turning their heads?
25) Who was the first U.S. president with a beard?

Quiz 22 Answers

1) Greenland – 836,300 square miles
2) The Hundred Years War
3) Oak
4) Alaska – It has about 365,000 miles of rivers.
5) Gregor Mendel
6) *When Harry Met Sally*
7) Aramis – the third musketeer in *The Three Musketeers*
8) *Jaws*
9) E
10) Sweden
11) Nelson Mandela
12) Switzerland
13) *Dune*
14) *The Exorcist* – 1973
15) Victoria
16) Oklahoma City and Indianapolis
17) Wiley Post – 1933
18) Liver - You can lose up to 75 percent of your liver, and the remaining portion can regenerate into a whole liver.
19) Sweden
20) Flyting - The exchange of insults could get quite rude, including accusations of cowardice or sexual perversion.
21) Istanbul, Turkey
22) Homer's *Odyssey*
23) Samuel Adams
24) Rabbit and parrot
25) Abraham Lincoln

Quiz 23

1) The density of what is measured on the Ringelmann Scale?
2) Who is the youngest ever world heavyweight boxing champion?
3) Who was the first person to cross the Antarctic Circle?
4) What was the first man-made object to break the sound barrier?
5) Who was the first Olympic boxing gold medalist to also win a boxing world championship?
6) What two planets in our solar system don't have moons?
7) Who had the only number-one song recorded by a father and daughter?
8) Who was the first woman to appear on a U.S. postage stamp?
9) By area, what is the largest body of freshwater in the world?
10) What book is subtitled *The Boy Who Wouldn't Grow Up*?
11) *The Aphrodite of Melos* has what better-known name?
12) Who is the only person to win Nobel Prizes in two different areas of science?
13) What is coulrophobia?
14) What is cartoon cat Garfield's favorite food?
15) What Canadian province borders the most states?
16) Based on the number of weeks at number one on Billboard's Hot 100, who was the top artist of the 1970s?
17) What lake is formed by the Hoover Dam?
18) Who was the first woman to win gold medals in two different sports at the same Winter Olympics?
19) Who wrote *Charlie and the Chocolate Factory*?
20) Until the 19th century, the word hypocrites referred to what profession?
21) What two countries share the island of New Guinea?
22) What condition is singultus?
23) What country has the longest land border?
24) What is the world's oldest monotheistic religion?
25) How long does it take the moon to revolve around the earth to the nearest day?

Quiz 23 Answers

1) Smoke
2) Mike Tyson – 20
3) Captain James Cook - 1773
4) Whip
5) Floyd Patterson – 1952 Olympics and 1956 world champion
6) Mercury and Venus
7) Frank and Nancy Sinatra – "Something Stupid" in 1967
8) Martha Washington - 1902
9) Lake Superior – 31,700 square miles
10) *Peter Pan*
11) *Venus de Milo*
12) Marie Curie – physics and chemistry
13) Fear of clowns
14) Lasagna
15) Ontario – borders Minnesota, Michigan, Ohio, Pennsylvania, New York
16) Bee Gees
17) Lake Mead
18) Ester Ledecka (Czech Republic) - 2018 PyeongChang Olympics in skiing and snowboarding
19) Roald Dahl
20) Actors
21) Indonesia and Papua New Guinea
22) Hiccups
23) China – 13,743 miles and 14 countries
24) Judaism
25) 27 days

Quiz 24

1) What is the oldest college football bowl game?
2) At the battle of Actium, who defeated Mark Antony and Cleopatra?
3) What city has the most skyscrapers in the world?
4) How many feet wide is a regulation NBA court?
5) On a pencil, what do the initials HB stand for?
6) What country eats the most donuts per capita?
7) What body part do frogs use to force food down their throats?
8) Timbuktu is in what country?
9) Who has the MLB record for most runs scored in a season?
10) Crocodiles don't sweat; what body part do they use to keep cool?
11) Written out in English, what is the first number alphabetically no matter how high you go?
12) Approximately 2% of all people have what eye color?
13) The Komodo dragon is native to what country?
14) Who won the most consecutive Wimbledon singles titles?
15) Astana is the capital of what country?
16) How many witches were burned at the stake during the Salem witch trials?
17) In 1911, Hiram Bingham discovered what?
18) Who is the only six-time winner (male or female) of the Associated Press Athlete of the year?
19) What is the more common name for an Einstein Rosen Bridge?
20) The Antoinette Perry Award for Excellence is better known as what?
21) What is Minnie Mouse's full first name?
22) The Tom Hanks movie *The Terminal* was inspired by a man who lived at the departure lounge of what international airport for 18 years?
23) What is the first color mentioned in the Bible?
24) What country has the most desert area in the world?
25) What country declared war on both Germany and the Allies in WWII?

Quiz 24 Answers

1) Rose Bowl – 1902
2) Octavian or Emperor Augustus
3) Hong Kong
4) 50 feet
5) Hard black
6) Canada – The presence of 3,000 Tim Hortons restaurants is a major factor.
7) Eyes - Since they don't have muscles to chew their food, they use their eyes to force food down their throats. Their eyes sink inside their skull to push the food down.
8) Mali – West Africa
9) Babe Ruth - 179 in 1921
10) Mouth - They open it like panting.
11) Eight
12) Green – Brown is 55%; hazel and blue are 8% each.
13) Indonesia
14) Martina Navratilova – six
15) Kazakhstan
16) None - Twenty were executed, but most were hung, and none were burned.
17) Lost city of Machu Picchu
18) Babe Didrikson Zaharias - 1932, 1945, 1946, 1947, 1950, 1954
19) Wormhole
20) Tony Award
21) Minerva
22) Charles de Gaulle Airport
23) Green
24) Australia - 965,000 square miles of desert
25) Italy – One month after surrendering to the allies, Italy declared war on Germany, its former ally.

Quiz 25

1) When accused of being two-faced, what U.S. president said, "If I had two faces, would I be wearing this one?"
2) Who was the first tennis player to win all four Grand Slam tournaments and an Olympic gold medal in the same calendar year?
3) Does the Northern Hemisphere or the Southern Hemisphere contain more of the world's land area?
4) What year were professionals allowed to compete in the Olympics?
5) A standard barrel of crude oil holds roughly how many gallons?
6) What kind of paint did Picasso use?
7) What is the only country that is exempt from the international rule that a country's name must appear on its postage stamps?
8) What are the five boroughs of New York City?
9) What element is named after a U.S. state?
10) Who was the first sitting U.S. president to visit Hiroshima?
11) A male donkey is called a jack; what is a female donkey called?
12) When a horse curls its upper lip and raises its head in the air, what is it trying to do?
13) In the electromagnetic spectrum, what comes between microwaves and visible light?
14) What is the world's largest gold depository?
15) Who performed the first heart transplant?
16) What famous scientist is credited as being the first person to put wheels on an office chair?
17) The Motel 6 and Super 8 motel chains both got their names from what?
18) What is the national animal of Scotland?
19) Who developed the system we use today for classifying plants and animals?
20) What country is Transylvania in?
21) What country has the oldest surviving constitution?
22) N_2O is more commonly known as what?
23) By area, what is the smallest of the Great Lakes?
24) What is the largest city on the Mississippi River?
25) What is an apparatus that converts molecules into ions and separates the ions according to their mass-to-charge ratio called?

Quiz 25 Answers

1) Abraham Lincoln
2) Steffi Graf – 1988
3) Northern Hemisphere – 68% of the total land
4) 1984
5) 42
6) House paint
7) Great Britain – They were the first country with postage stamps and had no name on them and were exempted when the rule was made.
8) Bronx, Queens, Staten Island, Manhattan, Brooklyn
9) Californium
10) Barack Obama
11) Jenny
12) Get a better smell - The behavior is called the flehmen response and is used to transfer inhaled scent molecules into the vomeronasal organ (VNO), a specialized chemosensory structure found in many mammals.
13) Infrared
14) Manhattan Federal Reserve Bank – about 6,700 tons
15) Dr. Christian Barnard
16) Charles Darwin – 1840
17) Their original room rates - Motel 6 charged $6 per night when it started in 1962, and Super 8 charged $8.88 per night when it started in 1974.
18) Unicorn
19) Carolus Linnaeus - In the first half of the 18th century, he developed a taxonomy for naming and classifying plants and animals.
20) Romania
21) San Marino – 1600
22) Laughing gas - nitrous oxide
23) Lake Ontario – 7,320 square miles
24) Memphis, Tennessee
25) Mass spectrometer

Quiz 26

1) What percent alcohol is 80 proof whiskey?
2) The Daleks from *Doctor Who* come from what planet?
3) What is the most visited U.S. city?
4) What is the name for the point in a planet's orbit when it is furthest from the sun?
5) What is the main visual difference between a monkey and an ape?
6) Besides elephants and rhinoceroses, what other animals are considered pachyderms?
7) What country invented french fried potatoes?
8) The Newbery Medal is given annually for what?
9) What plant produces about one-half of the earth's oxygen?
10) What is the only country to win a gold medal at every Winter Olympics?
11) What year was the first Super Bowl played?
12) In *The Lord of the Rings: The Fellowship of the Ring*, how many are in the original fellowship?
13) What name is given to the socket in the human skull that holds the eye?
14) Dalmatian dogs originated in what country?
15) What was the first man-made object in space?
16) In what movie does Marilyn Monroe's iconic scene with her white dress blowing upward while she stands on a subway grate take place?
17) What are the only two U.S. state capitals with rhyming names?
18) What is the international distress signal one level less serious than Mayday?
19) What country has the southernmost point in mainland Asia?
20) What 6th-century Greek poet is the father of drama?
21) The word orchid is Greek and literally means what?
22) By area, what is the smallest Central American country?
23) What 1990 movie was the first western to win the Best Picture Oscar in 59 years?
24) What classic novel is based on the adventures of Alexander Selkirk, an early 18th-century Scottish sailor?
25) What river flows through Baghdad, Iraq?

Quiz 26 Answers

1) 40%
2) Skaro
3) Orlando, Florida - New York City is second.
4) Aphelion
5) Monkeys have tails.
6) Hippopotamuses
7) Belgium - late 17th century
8) Best children's book
9) Phytoplankton
10) United States
11) 1967
12) Nine – Frodo, Gandalf, Legolas, Gimli, Aragorn, Boromir, Merry, Pippin, Samwise
13) Orbit
14) Croatia – Dalmatia region
15) German V2 rocket – 1942
16) *The Seven Year Itch* - 1955
17) Boston and Austin
18) Pan-Pan
19) Malaysia - Tanjung Piai at 1.3 degrees north latitude
20) Thespis
21) Testicle
22) El Salvador
23) *Dances with Wolves*
24) *Robinson Crusoe*
25) Tigris

Quiz 27

1) When a person is micturating, what are they doing?
2) Where are the Islands of Langerhans?
3) After Canada and Mexico, what country is closest to the United States?
4) What river has the largest drainage basin in the United States?
5) What are the only three countries that don't use the metric system?
6) Who was the only apostle of Jesus to die a natural death?
7) What is the longest-running animated children's show in the United States?
8) Thomas Edison was involved in a rivalry over which form of electricity would be commercialized; Edison supported direct current; who was his rival that supported alternating current?
9) In computing, what is half of a byte called?
10) What country's flag is incorporated most often in other flags?
11) What civilization first domesticated guinea pigs and used them for food, sacrifices, and household pets?
12) What are the dots on dice called?
13) Until it gained its independence in 1825, what country was known as Upper Peru?
14) What leader once ordered his army to eat every tenth man?
15) What is the second-most populous island in the world?
16) What team has the most consecutive NBA championships?
17) By volume, what is the largest freshwater lake?
18) What artist has the most consecutive number-one singles on Billboard's Hot 100?
19) The hominid or great ape family includes humans, gorillas, chimpanzees, and what?
20) What will be the first city to host both the summer and winter Olympics?
21) What was the first Disney animated feature film set in America?
22) What is the longest movie to ever win the Best Picture Oscar?
23) What is the effect of the earth's rotation on the wind called?
24) What is the southernmost city in the world with a population of over 10 million?
25) What is the name of the Greek goddess of victory?

Quiz 27 Answers

1) Urinating
2) Human pancreas – produce insulin
3) Russia – 2.4 miles
4) Mississippi River - It has a drainage basin of 1,245,000 square miles, including all or parts of 31 states.
5) United States, Liberia, Myanmar
6) Saint John
7) *Arthur* - started on PBS in 1996
8) Nikola Tesla
9) Nibble
10) Great Britain
11) Incas
12) Pips
13) Bolivia
14) Genghis Khan - In 1214, Khan was battling the Jin empire in China and laid siege to the city of Chengdu, capital of the Jin empire. The siege went on for a long time, and supplies were short; they were also ravaged by the plague. Khan ordered that every tenth man should be sacrificed to feed the others. Khan personally abandoned the siege, leaving it to one of his generals, and Chengdu eventually fell in 1215.
15) Honshu - Japan
16) Boston Celtics - eight from 1959–1966
17) Lake Baikal in Russia – It has a maximum depth of 5,387 feet and contains about 20% of the total unfrozen surface freshwater in the world.
18) Whitney Houston – seven
19) Orangutans
20) Beijing - 2008 summer and 2022 winter
21) *Dumbo*
22) *Gone with the Wind* - 238 minutes
23) Coriolis
24) Buenos Aires, Argentina - 34.6 degrees south latitude
25) Nike

Quiz 28

1) What pet did Florence Nightingale carry with her?
2) What was the first country to implement daylight saving time?
3) What was the first book Mark Twain published?
4) What state is the geographic center of North America?
5) What country has the lone sub-species of horse that is still entirely wild, having never been domesticated by humans?
6) In English, what is the shortest three-syllable word?
7) The nine-banded armadillo and humans have what in common?
8) Who wrote *Wuthering Heights*?
9) Which U.S. president established the Secret Service?
10) What was the first type of product sold in aerosol spray cans?
11) What is the brightest star in the night sky?
12) Who was the first woman to appear on the front of U.S. paper currency?
13) What ancient marvel did Nebuchadnezzar build?
14) What is the clotting protein in the blood called?
15) What was the first James Bond book?
16) What place on the earth is closest to the moon?
17) What is the deepest lake in Africa?
18) What is the only country in the world that doesn't have either a rectangular or square flag?
19) Who pitched the only no-hit game in World Series history?
20) What U.S. president was born as Leslie Lynch King Jr.?
21) What country has the highest percentage of natural redheads?
22) What river is Pocahontas buried along?
23) What two states share Lake Tahoe?
24) What singer did Elvis Presley say was the greatest in the world?
25) Outside of Warsaw, what city has the largest Polish population in the world?

Quiz 28 Answers

1) Owl – She carried it in her pocket.

2) Germany – in 1916 to save energy in WWI

3) *The Celebrated Jumping Frog of Calaveras County* - 1867

4) North Dakota

5) Mongolia - The endangered Przewalski's horse is native to the steppes of Mongolia; all other wild horses are feral horses that are descendants of domesticated horses.

6) W - The letters of the alphabet are generally also considered words since they are nouns referring to the letter.

7) Leprosy – They are the only animals known to be infected.

8) Emily Bronte

9) Abraham Lincoln - He established the Secret Service on the day he was assassinated, but it was originally only focused on counterfeiting and didn't protect the president until 1902 after McKinley's assassination.

10) Insecticide

11) Sirius – Dog Star

12) Martha Washington - She appeared on the $1 silver certificate in 1886.

13) Hanging Gardens of Babylon

14) Fibrin

15) *Casino Royale*

16) Mount Chimborazo, Ecuador – It is 20,548 feet high, but it is very close to the equator, so the bulge in the earth makes it 1.5 miles closer than Mount Everest.

17) Lake Tanganyika - 4,820 feet deep in southeastern Africa

18) Nepal - It has a combination of two triangular pennants.

19) Don Larsen – 1956

20) Gerald Ford

21) Scotland - about 13%

22) Thames River - England

23) California and Nevada

24) Roy Orbison

25) New York City

Quiz 29

1) What animal always gives birth to four identical offspring?

2) About 1 in every 200 people is born with an extra rib that forms above the first rib at the base of the neck just above the collarbone; what is it called?

3) What is a dactylogram?

4) $C_{10}H_{14}N_2$ is a poisonous alkaloid consumed by millions of people daily; what is it?

5) Outside of micro-organisms, what animal has existed the longest?

6) For what film did Audrey Hepburn win her only Oscar?

7) What U.S. state receives the least sunshine?

8) By area, how many of the world's 10 largest countries are in Asia?

9) What two U.S. states border Nevada to the north?

10) What mountain range passes through the most countries?

11) For what film did Steven Spielberg win his first Oscar?

12) In the ancient Olympics, women weren't allowed to participate or even be in the stadium, but they could still win the Olympic prize in what event?

13) What U.S. first lady was the first to also be the mother of a president?

14) What is the most frequently sold item at Walmart?

15) What country has the northernmost permanent settlement in the world?

16) What is the sunniest city in the world?

17) What sport originated the term home run?

18) If you include speed on land, in air, or in water, what is the fastest known mammal?

19) What was John Wayne's last movie?

20) What Oscar-winning actress was the Connecticut state golf champion at age 16?

21) What country has the easternmost point in Asia?

22) Who was the first female Speaker of the U.S. House of Representatives?

23) What is a group of rhinoceros called?

24) What is the highest-grossing romantic comedy film of all time?

25) What is the name for a male mule?

Quiz 29 Answers

1) Armadillo - A single embryo splits into four as part of their normal reproduction.

2) Cervical rib - You can have a cervical rib on either or both sides, and it can be a fully-formed bony rib or a thin strand of tissue fibers.

3) Fingerprint

4) Nicotine

5) Sponge - Fossils dating back 760 million years have been found.

6) *Roman Holiday*

7) Alaska

8) Four – Russia, China, India, Kazakhstan

9) Oregon and Idaho

10) Andes - seven countries - Venezuela, Colombia, Ecuador, Peru, Bolivia, Chile, Argentina

11) *Schindler's List*

12) Chariot racing - The prize went to the owner of the chariot and horse, so women could and did win the prize.

13) Abigail Adams

14) Bananas

15) Canada - Alert, Nunavut, Canada, is at 82.5 degrees north latitude, about 508 miles from the North pole

16) Yuma, Arizona – On average, the sun shines 90% of daylight hours.

17) Cricket

18) Mexican free-tailed bat – It can achieve speeds of 100 mph in normal flight.

19) *The Shootist* - 1976

20) Katharine Hepburn

21) Russia - Big Diomede at 169.1 degrees west longitude

22) Nancy Pelosi - 2007

23) Crash

24) *My Big Fat Greek Wedding* - 2002

25) John

Quiz 30

1) By area, what is the second-largest freshwater lake in the world?
2) How many U.S. states border Mexico?
3) What oil tanker was the cause of a massive oil spill in Alaska in 1989?
4) The aardvark is the first animal alphabetically; what's the second?
5) Who was condemned in Hades to forever push a boulder uphill, only for it to come rolling down before it reached the top?
6) What is Shakespeare's longest play?
7) What is the primary food for a koala?
8) What is the saltiest ocean?
9) Russia is the most populous country in Europe; what country is second?
10) What is the most visited urban park in the United States?
11) At normal atmospheric pressure, what is the only element in the universe that can't freeze?
12) What defines a blue moon?
13) Who was the oldest rookie in Major League Baseball at age 42?
14) Including tentacles, how many arms does a squid have?
15) What are Africa's four great rivers?
16) What planet in our solar system has a diameter just 397 miles smaller than the earth?
17) Who wrote *The Scarlet Letter*?
18) What year was the last time the Summer and Winter Olympics were held in the same year?
19) What Shakespeare play features the line "All the world's a stage, and all the men and women merely players"?
20) Who is the oldest acting Oscar winner?
21) Birds don't have what basic body function of most animals?
22) What do scientists believe is the most abundant vertebrate (animal with a backbone) species?
23) How many zeroes in a sextillion?
24) Scatomancy was popular in ancient Egypt; what is it?
25) What is the only Central American country that doesn't border the Caribbean Sea?

Quiz 30 Answers

1) Lake Victoria - 26,950 square miles
2) Four – California, Arizona, New Mexico, and Texas
3) *Exxon Valdez*
4) Aardwolf - It is native to eastern and southern Africa; it is a member of the hyena family and looks like a small striped hyena. It feeds on insects, primarily termites.
5) Sisyphus
6) Hamlet
7) Eucalyptus leaves
8) Atlantic
9) Germany
10) Central Park - New York City
11) Helium - Its freezing point is -458 degrees Fahrenheit.
12) The second full moon in a calendar month – It happens about every three years; thus, the expression "once in a blue moon" for something that doesn't occur very often.
13) Satchel Paige
14) 10 - two tentacles and eight arms
15) Nile, Congo, Zambezi, Niger
16) Venus
17) Nathaniel Hawthorne
18) 1992
19) *As You Like It*
20) Christopher Plummer – age 82 for best supporting actor in *Beginners* (2011)
21) They don't urinate. Birds convert excess nitrogen to uric acid instead of urea; it is less toxic and doesn't need to be diluted as much. It goes out with their other waste and saves water, so they don't have to drink as much.
22) Bristlemouth - They are small, deep-sea fish that are only about three inches long and usually live at depths exceeding 1,000 feet. They are believed to number in the quadrillions.
23) 21
24) Telling the future using someone's poop
25) El Salvador

Quiz 31

1) What U.S. president lived for 80 days after being shot?
2) What is the only African country that borders the Mediterranean Sea and the Red Sea?
3) The creature most people identify as a daddy-longlegs spider is not a spider at all; what is it?
4) What is a newly hatched swan called?
5) Who was the first U.S. president who didn't have any recognized biological children?
6) What body part does a cicada use to make its loud sound?
7) If something is napiform, it is shaped like what vegetable?
8) Which U.S. first lady was the first to win an Emmy Award?
9) Who is the only person to win four acting Oscars?
10) What character does Sean Hayes play on television's *Will & Grace*?
11) Who holds the NBA record for highest season points per game?
12) Who wrote the poem "The Song of Hiawatha"?
13) What current candy was part of U.S. soldier rations in WWII?
14) Lobsters have nozzles right under their eyes that they use to communicate with each other; what is released from the nozzles?
15) What year followed 1 BC?
16) Who is the Green Hornet's alter ego?
17) What color is most common on national flags?
18) What is the second-longest river in North America?
19) What single word is the opposite of extinct?
20) What are the two family names central to Shakespeare's *Romeo and Juliet*?
21) What was the name of Charles Darwin's survey ship?
22) What was Didus Ineptus better known as?
23) What is the world's most northerly national capital city?
24) Who was the first U.S. president born after WWII?
25) What animal has the largest eye?

Quiz 31 Answers

1) James A. Garfield
2) Egypt
3) Long-legged harvestmen - It is an arachnid but not a spider. Harvestmen have one body section instead of the two spiders have, two eyes instead of eight, a segmented body instead of unsegmented in spiders, no silk, no venom, and a different respiratory system than spiders, among other differences.
4) Cygnet
5) George Washington
6) Ribs - They flex their muscles to buckle a series of ribs one after another to produce their loud sound. Every time a rib buckles, it produces a click; many clicks produce the buzzing sound. The series of ribs are called a tymbal and can produce a sound over 100 decibels that can be heard over a mile and a half away.
7) Turnip
8) Jacqueline Kennedy - She won a Trustees Award for a 1962 televised tour of the White House.
9) Katharine Hepburn
10) Jack McFarland
11) Wilt Chamberlain - 50.4 ppg in 1961-62 season
12) Henry Wadsworth Longfellow
13) Tootsie Rolls - They were durable in all weather conditions and were good for quick energy.
14) Urine
15) 1 AD
16) Britt Reed
17) Red
18) Mississippi River – 2,320 miles
19) Extant
20) Capulets and Montagues
21) Beagle
22) Dodo bird
23) Reykjavik, Iceland – 64 degrees north latitude
24) Bill Clinton
25) Giant and colossal squid - up to an 11-inch diameter

Quiz 32

1) If an animal is oviparous, what does it do?
2) What is the lowest average elevation continent?
3) What was Queen Victoria's first name?
4) What country is the largest wine producer in the world?
5) What state borders Alabama to the west?
6) What is the word for the third to the last thing?
7) In 1944's movie *National Velvet*, what is the name of Velvet Brown's horse?
8) What London club does Mycroft Holmes belong to?
9) There is a chunk of Africa stuck under the United States from when the supercontinent Pangaea broke apart about 250 million years ago. It is located off the coast nearest to what state?
10) What other animals besides humans have chins?
11) By area, what is the largest country in the world without any mountains (points greater than 2,000 feet elevation)?
12) English is the official language of more countries than any other language; what is the second most popular official language?
13) How many pairs of legs does a shrimp have?
14) What is the least accessible U.S. state capital?
15) What movie has the line "I love the smell of napalm in the morning"?
16) Who was the first tennis player to achieve the calendar year grand slam?
17) What element has the lowest boiling point?
18) Edgar Allan Poe created mystery fiction's first detective in what 1841 story?
19) What animal is the source of the Middle East Respiratory Syndrome (MERS) virus and is also likely the source of the common cold?
20) What is the world's oldest currency still in use?
21) What letter starts the most words in the English language?
22) What is Britain's largest native carnivore?
23) Vulpine relates to what kind of animal?
24) What is Australia's island state?
25) What country invented the crossbow?

Quiz 32 Answers

1) Lay eggs - There is no embryonic development inside the mother.
2) Australia – 984 feet average elevation
3) Alexandrina
4) Italy - followed by Spain, France, United States
5) Mississippi
6) Antepenultimate
7) The Pie
8) Diogenes
9) Alabama
10) None - Humans are the only animal with a chin; no one knows why.
11) Belarus - 80,155 square miles with a maximum elevation of 1,130 feet
12) French - 29 countries
13) Five
14) Juneau, Alaska – You must fly or take a boat.
15) *Apocalypse Now* - 1979
16) Don Budge – 1938
17) Helium – negative 452.1 degrees Fahrenheit
18) *The Murders in the Rue Morgue*
19) Camel
20) British pound – 1,200 years
21) S
22) Badger
23) Foxes
24) Tasmania
25) China – about 700 BC

Quiz 33

1) What animal causes 10%-20% of all power outages in the United States?
2) The Borg-Warner Trophy is awarded for winning what?
3) Who was the first U.S. president to die in office?
4) What is the only U.S. state that is at least three states or provinces away from the ocean in every direction?
5) What is parthenogenesis?
6) What is the cultivation of grapes known as?
7) What were golf balls originally made of?
8) What do you call a group of unicorns?
9) What is Eddie Murphy's character name in the movie *Beverly Hills Cop*?
10) What is the fleshy end of your nose that splits your nostrils called?
11) What country has the world's heaviest building?
12) The Eiffel Tower wasn't intended to be permanent; it was scheduled for demolition in 1909 but was saved to be used as what?
13) What is probably the closest thing to a universal word because it means the same thing in every language and everybody in almost every language says it?
14) The European organization for nuclear research is known by what four letters?
15) What explorer's last words were "I have not told half of what I saw"?
16) In what country did chocolate originate?
17) Who was the first American in space?
18) Who was the first president depicted on a circulating U.S. monetary coin?
19) What animal has the greatest bite force?
20) If you have a case of pronoia; what is it?
21) By area, what is the world's largest freshwater island?
22) Characters such as those in Chinese where a word is represented by a picture are called what?
23) What can't rats do that makes them particularly vulnerable to poison?
24) By volume, what is the second-largest freshwater lake in the world?
25) What is the largest island in the world formed solely by volcanic activity?

Quiz 33 Answers

1) Squirrel - Squirrel outages tend to be more localized and more quickly fixed than those caused by storms.
2) Indianapolis 500
3) William Henry Harrison - 1841
4) Nebraska
5) Asexual reproduction – In animals, it equates to a virgin birth.
6) Viticulture
7) Wood - In the early 17th century, wood was replaced by a feather ball consisting of boiled feathers compressed inside a stitched leather cover.
8) A blessing
9) Axel Foley
10) Columella nasi
11) Romania - The Palace of Parliament in Bucharest is 275.6 feet high and covers an area of 1.41 square miles with a volume of 2.55 million cubic meters and weighs about 9 billion pounds. It is the second-largest building in the world by surface area.
12) Radio tower
13) Huh
14) CERN – from the French "Conseil Europeen pour la Recherche Nucleaire"
15) Marco Polo
16) Mexico
17) Alan Shepard Jr. - 1961
18) Abraham Lincoln
19) Nile crocodile – 5,000 psi
20) Opposite of paranoia – feeling that a conspiracy exists to help you
21) Manitoulin – over 1,000 square miles in Lake Huron in Ontario, Canada
22) Ideograms
23) Vomit
24) Tanganyika – maximum depth of 4,820 feet
25) Iceland – 39,768 square miles

Quiz 34

1) What is the most abundant metal in the earth's crust?
2) What is the only host country not to win a gold medal at its own summer Olympics?
3) In the movies, what was Charles Foster Kane's dying word?
4) What Shakespeare play ends in the marriage of Benedick and Beatrice?
5) What country landed the first man-made object on the moon?
6) What golfer holds the record for most PGA tour wins in a season?
7) What is the fastest growing plant?
8) By area, what is the largest lake in Africa?
9) By population, what is the largest city entirely in Europe?
10) How many Olympics have been hosted in Africa?
11) What is the most commonly used noun in the English language?
12) If you are locked in a completely sealed room, what will kill you first?
13) What is the hardest substance in the human body?
14) Who holds the NBA career record for most steals?
15) What is the opposite of nocturnal?
16) Who is the only U.S. president to serve two nonconsecutive terms?
17) Who was the first U.S. president born in the 20th century?
18) What is the southernmost national capital city in North America?
19) The word deadline originated in what war?
20) Who broke the world record over 30 times in the pole vault?
21) What two countries have the second-longest shared land border?
22) What country consumes the most fish per capita?
23) Who were the first NFL quarterback and running back teammates to each rush for 1,000 yards in the same season?
24) What country has the westernmost point in Asia?
25) What civilization was the first to divide the day into 24 hours?

Quiz 34 Answers

1) Aluminum
2) Canada – Montreal Olympics in 1976
3) Rosebud
4) *Much Ado About Nothing*
5) Soviet Union – *Luna 2* in 1959
6) Byron Nelson – 18 wins in 1945
7) Bamboo – Some species can grow three feet in a day.
8) Victoria – 26,564 square miles
9) Moscow, Russia
10) Zero
11) Time
12) Carbon dioxide poisoning – It will kill you before you die from lack of oxygen.
13) Tooth enamel
14) John Stockton – 3,265
15) Diurnal
16) Grover Cleveland – 22nd and 24th president
17) John F. Kennedy
18) Panama City, Panama – 9 degrees north latitude
19) American Civil War – In Civil War prison camps, it was the line that prisoners couldn't go beyond, or they would be shot.
20) Sergey Bubka
21) Russia and Kazakhstan – 4,254 miles
22) Iceland
23) Michael Vick and Warrick Dunn – 2006 Atlanta Falcons
24) Turkey – Cape Baba at 26.1 degrees east longitude
25) Egyptian – Ancient Egyptians used a base 12 system instead of our base 10 system; they counted the knuckles of each finger using their thumbs as pointers. They had 12 hours of light and 12 hours of darkness, so the length of the hours varied by time of the year. Fixed length hours were proposed by the Greeks in the 2nd century BC, but they did not become common until mechanical clocks first appeared in Europe during the 14th century.

Quiz 35

1) What is the deepest canyon in the United States?

2) What comedian had the first comedy album ever to hit number one?

3) What city has the world's busiest McDonald's restaurant?

4) Roman gladiator fights started as a part of what ceremony?

5) What was Alfred Hitchcock's only Best Picture Oscar winner?

6) What was Charles Dickens's first novel?

7) What poet wrote, "I have promises to keep, and miles to go before I sleep"?

8) Dire wolves, as seen in *Game of Thrones*, existed up to about 10,000 years ago on what continents?

9) Who wrote *2001: A Space Odyssey*?

10) What do the words uncopyrightable and dermatoglyphics have in common?

11) Who created Winnie the Pooh?

12) What are the monkeys Mizaru, Kikazaru, and Iwazaru better known as?

13) By area, what is the largest island in Asia?

14) What is the only music group where every member has written more than one number-one single?

15) What male fish species give birth?

16) By area, what is the second smallest U.S. state?

17) What is the study of bumps on the head called?

18) By area, what is the smallest North American country?

19) What country has the largest Muslim population?

20) What is the highest mountain in the United States?

21) In what country did volleyball originate?

22) Outside of Asia, what is the highest mountain range in the world?

23) The end of the Pony Express line was in what western city?

24) What MLB pitcher has the most career losses?

25) Who wrote, "Poems are made by fools like me, but only God can make a tree"?

Quiz 35 Answers

1) Kings Canyon - maximum depth of 8,200 feet in California
2) Bob Newhart – *The Button-Down Mind of Bob Newhart* in 1960
3) Moscow, Russia
4) Funerals – When wealthy nobles died, they would have bouts at the graveside.
5) *Rebecca* – 1940
6) *The Pickwick Papers*
7) Robert Frost
8) North and South America - They were about the same size as the largest modern gray wolves, at about 150 pounds on average, but their teeth were larger with greater shearing ability, and they had the highest bite force of any known Canis species.
9) Arthur C. Clarke
10) Longest English words with no repeated letters
11) A.A. Milne
12) See No Evil, Hear No Evil, Speak No Evil
13) Borneo – 287,000 square miles
14) Queen - All four members have been inducted into the Songwriters Hall of Fame.
15) Seahorse and pipefish
16) Delaware - 2,489 square miles
17) Phrenology
18) St. Kitts and Nevis – 101 square miles in the Caribbean
19) Indonesia
20) Denali or Mount McKinley, Alaska – 20,310 feet
21) United States
22) Andes - maximum elevation of 22,841 feet
23) Sacramento, California
24) Cy Young – 316 losses
25) Joyce Kilmer

Quiz 36

1) What is the bloodiest single day of battle in U.S. history?
2) Who wrote *Of Mice and Men*?
3) What is the warmest ocean?
4) In *The Hunger Games*, what is the name of the futuristic nation?
5) Who was the first film star to earn 1 million dollars for a single film?
6) Who wrote "The Gift of the Magi" and is known for his surprise endings?
7) Who is the largest toy distributor in the world?
8) By area, what is the largest island nation?
9) Beriberi disease is caused by a deficiency of what vitamin?
10) What television show has the most Emmy wins for a drama?
11) In *The Jungle Book*, what is the name of the bear?
12) In the 48 contiguous U.S. states, what is the most northern state capital?
13) What country has four of the five highest circulation newspapers in the world?
14) What is the name for a group of mosquitoes?
15) What animal has the most legs?
16) What MLB player has the career record for the most total bases?
17) What Roman measurement is 1,500 paces?
18) What does DC stand for in DC Comics?
19) The minnow is the smallest member of what fish family?
20) Under the original terms of the U.S. Constitution, the president didn't choose his vice president; how was it decided?
21) What is the only U.S. city to win three of the four major professional sports championships in the same year?
22) What U.S. president was arrested and taken into custody for speeding with a horse and buggy in Washington D.C. while he was in office?
23) What was the first food product tested in a microwave oven?
24) What is unique about a palmiped animal?
25) What part of the eye continues to grow throughout a person's life?

Quiz 36 Answers

1) Battle of Antietam in the American Civil War - 22,000 dead, wounded, or missing
2) John Steinbeck
3) Indian Ocean
4) Panem
5) Elizabeth Taylor - *Cleopatra* in 1963
6) O. Henry
7) McDonald's – About 20% of its meals are Happy Meals with a toy.
8) Indonesia – 735,358 square miles
9) B1 - thiamine
10) *Game of Thrones* (2011–2019) – 59 wins
11) Baloo
12) Olympia, Washington
13) Japan
14) Scourge
15) Millipede – up to 750
16) Hank Aaron - 6,856 bases
17) League
18) Detective Comics
19) Carp or cyprinid
20) The candidate with the second most electoral votes was the vice president.
21) Detroit – 1935, won NFL, NBA, and NHL
22) Ulysses S. Grant - The police seized his horse and buggy; he paid a fine and walked back to the White House.
23) Popcorn
24) Web–footed
25) Lens

Quiz 37

1) Who is the oldest person ever to go into space?

2) When Thomas Jefferson sent Lewis and Clark on their expedition, what extinct animal did he ask them to look for?

3) What national park has the nickname "Crown of the Continent"?

4) What animal produces its own sunscreen?

5) What common clothing item comes from the Persian for "leg garment"?

6) By area, what is the second-largest island nation in the world?

7) What is the pleasant odor after a rain called?

8) What are the colors of the five rings on the Olympic flag?

9) What country has the world's largest rock?

10) What is the most poached (illegally hunted) animal in the world?

11) What is the heaviest web-footed bird?

12) What were table tennis balls originally made from?

13) What ingredient makes vinegar taste sour or bitter?

14) What is measured on the Gay-Lussac scale?

15) What is the largest nerve in the human body?

16) What NASA space flight was the last manned mission to the moon?

17) What U.S. president collected *Spiderman* and *Conan the Barbarian* comic books?

18) Walnuts, almonds, pecans, and cashews aren't technically nuts; what are they?

19) The syrinx allows birds to do what?

20) Of all the animal species scientists have studied, what is the only one that shows no outward signs of conciliatory behavior?

21) Where in the human body is the labyrinth?

22) What is the most visited city in the world?

23) What is the name of the gypsy girl Quasimodo falls in love with in *The Hunchback of Notre Dame*?

24) What U.S. president hated public speaking and only made two speeches that were both inaugural speeches and hardly audible during his entire eight-year presidency?

25) What is the common name for the fruit Citrus grandis?

Quiz 37 Answers

1) John Glenn – 77
2) Wooly mammoth - Jefferson believed that there might be wooly mammoths still living in the west.
3) Glacier National Park
4) Hippopotamus – They produce a mucus-like secretion that keeps them cool and acts as a powerful sunscreen.
5) Pajamas
6) Madagascar - 226,658 square miles
7) Petrichor
8) Blue, yellow, black, green, red
9) Australia - Mount Augustus in the Australian Outback is 2,350 feet high and 5 miles long, occupying an area of about 18.5 square miles. It is about 2.5 times larger than Ayers Rock.
10) Pangolin - It is a small mammal covered in large overlapping scales that eats ants and termites and is generally found in Asia and sub-Saharan Africa. It is poached for its scales, which are used in traditional medicine, and for its meat.
11) Emperor penguin - up to 100 pounds
12) Cork – from wine bottles
13) Acetic acid – Vinegar typically contains 5-20% acetic acid.
14) Alcohol strength
15) Sciatic
16) *Apollo 17*
17) Barack Obama
18) Drupes – They also include peaches, plums, and cherries. Drupes are a type of fruit where an outer fleshy part surrounds a shell or pit with a seed inside.
19) Sing - It is their vocal organ.
20) Domestic cat
21) Ear
22) Bangkok, Thailand
23) Esmeralda
24) Thomas Jefferson
25) Grapefruit

Quiz 38

1) In 1917, Janette Rankin become the first woman in the United States to do what?
2) In *Star Wars*, what is the name of Princess Leia's home planet?
3) Who was the first U.S. president born a citizen of the United States?
4) In what country was the famous Rumble in the Jungle boxing match between Muhammad Ali and George Foreman fought?
5) Why are pencils typically yellow?
6) How many landlocked countries are there in North America?
7) What was the first group to appear in Madame Tussauds Wax Museum as waxwork models?
8) Who was the first person to win Oscars for both acting and writing?
9) What was the most-watched U.S. television series finale of all time?
10) In its natural form, aspirin comes from the bark of what tree?
11) The gender of most turtles, alligators, and crocodiles is determined after fertilization by what?
12) What Quentin Tarantino movie is about two mob hitmen, a boxer, a gangster's wife, and a pair of diner bandits?
13) What was the first U.S. number-one hit for the Beatles?
14) What country has the southernmost point in North America?
15) What globally successful product was created by Dr. John Pemberton?
16) How many movements traditionally make up a concerto?
17) Armadillos are good swimmers, but what other method do they use to cross bodies of water?
18) Who was the first person to win Emmys for acting, writing, and directing for the same television series?
19) The New Testament was originally written in what language?
20) What U.S. president believed the earth's core was hollow and signed off on an expedition to explore it?
21) What television show cast holds the record for most Billboard Hot 100 hit song entries?
22) What sense is most closely linked to memory?
23) What country's phone book is alphabetized by first name?
24) The 1964 Nobel Peace Prize was awarded to its youngest recipient up to that point; who was it?
25) What country has the northernmost point in South America?

Quiz 38 Answers

1) Elected to the U.S. Congress

2) Alderaan

3) Martin Van Buren

4) Zaire

5) It is the traditional color of Chinese royalty. In the 1890s when pencils started to be mass-produced, the best graphite came from China. Manufacturers wanted people to know they used the best quality graphite, so they painted them yellow, the color of Chinese royalty.

6) Zero

7) Beatles

8) Emma Thompson – Best Actress Oscar for *Howards End* (1992) and Best Adapted Screenplay Oscar for *Sense and Sensibility* (1995)

9) *M*A*S*H*

10) White willow tree

11) The temperature of the eggs decides whether the offspring will be male or female. This is called temperature-dependent sex determination.

12) *Pulp Fiction* – 1994

13) "I Want to Hold Your Hand"

14) Costa Rica - Cocos Island at 5.5 degrees north latitude

15) Coca-Cola

16) Three

17) They walk underwater; they can hold their breath for six to eight minutes.

18) Alan Alda - *M*A*S*H*

19) Greek

20) John Quincy Adams - The expedition never took place.

21) *Glee* (2009-2015) - 207 entries

22) Smell

23) Iceland – Everyone is referenced by their first name; they don't have surnames in the traditional sense; their surname is their father's first name suffixed with either son or daughter.

24) Martin Luther King Jr. – age 35

25) Colombia - Santa Catalina Island at 13.4 degrees north latitude

Quiz 39

1) By area, what is the largest country that the equator passes through?
2) What is the only non-rectangular U.S. state flag?
3) What novelist is known as the father of science fiction?
4) What is the oldest college in the United States?
5) What are the most luminous objects in the known universe?
6) Who was the last U.S. president who wasn't either a Democrat or Republican?
7) What desert contains the largest continuous body of sand in the world?
8) The movie *A Christmas Story* is based on what writer's work?
9) Who was the last British monarch to ascend to the throne as a teenager?
10) What country's flag has lasted the longest without change?
11) Iosif Vissarionovich Dzhugashvili became famous under what name?
12) Who was the first *Time* magazine man of the year?
13) What is the tallest mountain in the known universe?
14) What is the second largest bird in the world and is also considered the most dangerous bird?
15) Who was the first member of the British royal family to graduate from a university?
16) What is the only number spelled out in English that has its letters in alphabetical order?
17) What was the last U.S. television show to have its entire run filmed in black and white?
18) Who was the first U.S. president who was a Boy Scout?
19) What is the longest-running television show of any kind in the United States?
20) Gunpowder is made up of a mixture of sulfur, charcoal, and what?
21) What gas is the second most common in the earth's atmosphere?
22) What sport was transferred from the Summer Olympics to the Winter Olympics in 1924?
23) Because of the speed the sun moves at, what is the maximum possible length for a solar eclipse to the nearest minute?
24) What hockey player has won the most Stanley Cups?
25) Who was King of Mycenae and commander of the Greek forces in the Trojan War?

Quiz 39 Answers

1) Brazil
2) Ohio – swallowtail design
3) Jules Verne
4) Harvard – 1636
5) Quasars - They are highly luminous radio galaxies with a supermassive black hole; the nearest known quasar is 600 million light-years away.
6) Millard Fillmore – 1850
7) Arabian Desert - The contiguous sand body within it is known as the Rub 'al-Khali or the "Empty Quarter" and is about 250,966 square miles.
8) Jean Shepherd
9) Queen Victoria - She was 18 when she became queen in 1837.
10) Denmark – 1370 or earlier
11) Joseph Stalin
12) Charles Lindbergh – 1927
13) Olympus Mons on Mars – 69,459 feet
14) Cassowary - They are up to 6 feet tall and weigh up to 130 pounds and have a 4-inch, dagger-like claw on each foot that can slice open a predator or threat with a single kick. They are native to the tropical forests of Papua New Guinea, Indonesia, and northeastern Australia.
15) Prince Charles
16) Forty
17) *The Dick Van Dyke Show* (1961-1966)
18) John F. Kennedy
19) *Meet the Press* – started in 1947 and still running
20) Potassium nitrate
21) Oxygen - about 21%
22) Ice hockey
23) Eight minutes - 7 minutes and 58 seconds
24) Henri Richard – 11 with the Montreal Canadiens
25) Agamemnon

Quiz 40

1) Ski jumping and cross-country skiing are combined into what Olympic sport?
2) In the *Lethal Weapon* movies, what is Mel Gibson's character name?
3) What country would you have to visit to see the ruins of Troy?
4) What was the first U.S. college sport to name an All-American team?
5) What NHL player has the second most career regular-season points?
6) Who is the only U.S. president to be the grandson of another president?
7) Who made his film debut as Boo Radley in *To Kill a Mockingbird*?
8) What U.S. state has the highest percentage of its population that is foreign-born?
9) In what country is the only point on the equator with snow on the ground?
10) What is the least densely populated country in the world?
11) The Anatolian peninsula makes up most of what country?
12) What is the only animal with two kneecaps on each knee?
13) What bird has the largest wingspan?
14) What is the highest mountain range in North America?
15) What country has the largest population of poisonous snakes?
16) What is the world's warmest sea?
17) In the 48 contiguous U.S. states, what is the most southern state capital?
18) What country invented cheesecake?
19) What are the four states of matter observable in everyday life?
20) What was the first pizza chain in the United States?
21) Fireflies are what kind of insect?
22) What is the largest country that uses only one time zone?
23) What is the world's oldest golf course?
24) Whose image is engraved on the Pulitzer Prize gold medals?
25) Who wrote the song "I Will Always Love You"?

Quiz 40 Answers

1) Nordic combined
2) Martin Riggs
3) Turkey
4) Football – 1889
5) Jaromir Jagr - 1,921 points
6) Benjamin Harrison - grandson of William Henry Harrison
7) Robert Duvall
8) California
9) Ecuador
10) Mongolia – Areas like Greenland have an even lower density, but they aren't independent countries.
11) Turkey
12) Ostrich
13) Albatross – up to over 11 feet
14) Alaska Range - 20,343 feet maximum elevation
15) Australia
16) Red Sea
17) Austin, Texas
18) Greece
19) Solid, liquid, gas, plasma
20) Pizza Hut - 1958
21) Beetle
22) China – Geographically, it has five time zones, but it chooses to use one standard time.
23) St. Andrews, Scotland
24) Benjamin Franklin
25) Dolly Parton

Anything and Everything

If you enjoyed this book and learned a little and would like others to enjoy it also, please put out a review or rating. If you scan the QR code below, it will take you directly to the Amazon review and rating page.